glowing enigmas

SELECTED TRANSLATIONS
BY MICHAEL HAMBURGER

Poems of Hölderlin

Twenty Prose Poems, Charles Baudelaire

Letters, Journals and Conversations, Ludwig van Beethoven

Decline, Georg Trakl

The Burnt Offering, Albrecht Goes

Tales from the Calendar, Bertolt Brecht

Poems and Verse Plays, Hugo von Hofmannsthal

Modern German Poetry 1910-1960

Selected Verse, Friedrich Hölderlin

Selected Poems, Nelly Sachs

The Poems of Hans Magnus Enzensberger

Poems for People Who Don't Read Poems, Hans Magnus Enzensberger

An Unofficial Rilke

Poems, Paul Celan

Selected Poems and Fragments, Friedrich Hölderlin

After Nature, W. G. Sebald

Unrecounted, W. G. Sebald

glowing enigmas

NELLY SACHS

TRANSLATED FROM THE GERMAN BY

MICHAEL HAMBURGER

TAVERN BOOKS

P O R T L A N D

Printed in the United States of America.

Cover Art: Sarah Horowitz, *Chrysalis*, 2011. Ink drawing.
Copyright © Sarah Horowitz. Courtesy of the artist.

Author Photo ("Nelly Sachs, 1960"): Anna Riwkin.
Courtesy of the Moderna Museet, Stockholm.

Hamburger, Michael, 1924-2007
Sachs, Nelly, 1891-1970

ISBN-13: 978-1-935635-22-2 (paperback)
ISBN-13: 978-1-935635-27-7 (hardcover)

LCCN: 2012952608

FIRST EDITION

98765432 First Printing

TAVERN BOOKS
Portland, Oregon
www.tavernbooks.com

contents

glowing enigmas

I

This night
I turned the corner into
a dark side street
Then my shadow
lay down in my arm
This tired piece of clothing
wanted to be carried
and the color Nothing addressed me:
You are beyond!

Up and down I walk
in the room's warmth
The mad people in the corridor screech
together with the black birds outside
about the future
Our wounds blast this evil time
but slowly the clocks tick—

Doing nothing
perceptible wilting
My hands belong to a wingbeat stolen and carried off
With them I am sewing around a hole
but they sigh before this open abyss—

I wash my clothes
Much dying sings in the shift
here and there the counterpoint death
The pursuers have threaded in
together with the hypnosis
and the material absorbs it willingly in sleep—

Effulgence of lights enters into the dark verse
blows with the banner called understanding
I am to go out and search horror
Finding is elsewhere—

Behind the door
you pull on the rope of longing
till tears come
In this wellspring you're mirrored—

Here we wind a wreath
Some have violets of thunder
I have only a blade of grass
full of the silent language
that makes this air flash—

Only death draws out of them the truth of misery
these recurring rhymes cut out of night's blackness
these tongue exercises
at the end of the organ of sounds—

This telegraphy measures with the mathematics à la satane
the sensitively music-making places
in my body
An angel builds from the desires of love
dies and rises again in the letters
in which I travel—

If now you desperately call the one name
out of the darkness—
Wait a moment longer—
and you walk upon the sea
Already the element transfuses your pores
you are lowered with it and lifted
and found again soon in the sand
and on the stars an awaited guest arriving by air
and consumed in the fire of reunion

be still—be still—

Time's pasture cropped
on the amber of your face
The night thunderstorm approaches flaming
but the rainbow
already is stretching its colors
on to the convex surface of comfort—

Those who live on have clutched at time
until gold dust was left on their hands
They sing sun—sun—
midnight the dark eye
has been covered with the shroud—

Solitude of silent velvety fields
of violas
abandoned by red and blue
violet the going color
your weeping creates it
from the delicate fear of your eyes—

You have misplaced your name
but the world comes running
to offer you a good selection
You shake your head
but your lover
once found your needle for you in a haystack
Listen: he's calling already—

The beds are being made for pain
The linen is pain's close friend
It wrestles with the archangel
who never discards his invisibility
Breath weighed down with stones looks for new ways out
but the crucified star
falls again and again like windfalls
on to pain's shawl—

When I come to leave the room protected by illness
free to live—to die—
air with its welcoming kiss
deeply delights the twin mouth
then I shall not know
what my invisible
will do with me now—

You speak with me in the night
but fought off like all the dead
you have left the last letter
and the music of throats
to earth
that sings farewell up and down all the scales
But bedded in the blown sand
I hear new sounds in grace—

Princesses of sadness
who fishes out your sorrows?
Where do the funerals take place?
What ocean straits weep for you
with the embrace of an inner homeland?

Night your sister
takes leave of you
as the last lover—

Forgive me my sisters
I have taken your silence into my heart
There it lives and suffers the pearls of your suffering
heartache knocks
so loud so piercingly shrill
A lioness rides on the waves of Oceana
a lioness of pains
that long ago gave her tears to the sea—

Quickly death is removed from sight
The elements riot
but the budding spheres
already press in with resurrection
and that which is wordless heals the ailing star—

Weep away the unleashed heaviness of fear
Two butterflies support the weight of the world for you
and I lay your tears into these words:
Your fear has begun to shine—

In one moment a star closes its eye
The toad loses its moonstone
You in your bed give your breath to night
O map of the universe
Your signs show the veins of strangeness
out of our minds—

Disinherited we weep for dust—

My love flowed out into your martyrdom
broke through death
We live in resurrection—

In the bewitched wood
with the peeled-off bark of existence
where footprints bleed
glowing enigmas gaze at each other
intercept messages
from grave vaults—

Behind them
appears the second vision
the secret pact has been made—

Sick people are about to recapture
wild beasts that broke out of their blood—
Going out to hunt with their eyes
to that place where day
lies in colors startled by death
and the depth of the moon
enters their wide-open hibernation
sharply drawing them upward
until the thread of earth breaks
and they hang on the snow apple
their limbs beating—

My beloved dead
a hair made of darkness even
is called remoteness
softly grows through open time
I die filling a secret measure
into the minute
that budding stretches
but behind my back they have planted
the tongues of fire on to the earth—
A vine that yields its juice to the flame
I sink back—

As I wait here
time yearns out at sea
but is pulled back again and again by its blue hair
does not reach eternity—
Still no love between the planets
but a secret understanding already quivers—

A bleeding away wide as the evening
till darkness digs the grave
embryo of the dream in the womb
knocks
Creative air slowly covers itself
with the skin of new birth
Pain inscribes itself
with the fan of visions
life and death go on—

New Flood again and again
with those letters brought out by torture
those fishes that speak on the hook
in the skeleton of salt
to make legible the wound—

To learn dying again and again
from the old life
flight through the door of air
to fetch new sin from sleeping planets
Extreme exercise upon the old element
of breathing
startled by new death
What became of the tear
when earth vanished?

They speak snow—
The cloth of hours with its four cosmic ends
bears itself in
war and flight to the stars crouch next to each other
look for asylum where night
overflows with mother's milk
and beckons with a black finger
where new discoveries await the soul explorers
sparkling in darkness
deep underneath the snow—

II

Visions all dusk
lost things of the dead
we also leave to the newly born
what in us is most lonely—

Someone turns round
and peers into the desert—
hallucination opens
the wall of sun wilderness
where an ancestral couple
speaks the language of dust unveiled
remote as a conch, and sealed—

we freeze
and grapple with the next pace
into what's to come—

Always empty time
is hungry
for the inscription of transitoriness—
Furled into night's banner
with all the marvels
we know nothing
save that your loneliness
is not mine—
perhaps a dream-attained green
or
a song
from prebirth can glisten
and from the bridges of sighs of our speech
we hear the secret roar of the deeps—

Pavement—cars—feet
who now remembers that he roams a star
that he stands on a caldron of flames
with greedy tongues impatient to break through
that his step touches the geology of nights

When the man seduced by sleep
rises
guilt-laden
from the wellshaft of morning
he does not know
that he is wrapped in the nightclothes of the chrysalis
for still he has not experienced his prebirth
nor abandoned himself to his death

All's metamorphosis
flutters the butterfly—

Premonitions
wandering ears of corn
on a black field—
lie beside me
emigrated—airy—
lifeless discovery of a beyond
Two to One
or None—
the laws consumed in the lightning of stillness
at the rim leaning out
over my life laid on its bier—

In the interim
love at times takes trips into brightness
that smashes to smithereens
all protecting night

Trumpet
Light of Judgment Day
the body quivers with eagles' wings
carried off too high—

Under my foot all the countries
have rooted their great terrors
that hang heavy-ancient wells
always overfilling evening
the killing word—

I cannot be like that
only in falling—

If I close my eyes
suns push their time
leaving golden homes
yet inhabiting them
Mineral knows the way
to saved-up eternity
no longer passable
save unconscious in love—

In the sea of minutes
each one demands destruction
rescue-help high as houses interlaced with words
no longer air
only destruction
spaceless
only destruction
Hope became no butterfly
to create death with so much effort
Dissolve in sand
that which veils the God
this first word
that rushes into night
beyond rescuing

Earth
Tear among the planets—
I go down in your plenty—

So deep I traveled down
beyond my birth
till I met early death
that sent me back again
into this singing pyramid
to survey the inflamed
realm of silence
and whitely I crave you
death—be no stepfather to me now—

When the great terror came
I fell dumb—
Fish with its deathly side
turned upward
air bubbles paid for the grappling breath

All words in flight
to their immortal hiding places
where creative power has to spell
its planetary births
and time loses its knowledge
to the enigmas of light—

Straight into the uttermost
no hide and seek with pain
I can only look for you
if I fill my mouth with sand
so as to taste resurrection
for you have left my sorrow
from my love you have departed
you my beloved—

Only where find those words
those illumined by the first sea
those opening their eyes
those not wounded by tongues
those hidden by the light-wise
for your inflamed ascension
those words
which a universe piloted into silence
draws along with it into your Springs—

Still wound about the forehead
the strict horizon of illness
with the raving revolt of conflict—
the lifeline cast into the chasm
to hold one drowning in night—

O-A-O-A-
a rocking sea of vowels
all the words have crashed down—

Already your being's paradigm
has grown into your beyond
long yearned for distantly
in that place where smiling and weeping
become foundlings in the invisible
the images of vision given away to what's higher—

But you pressed down the keys
into their graves of music
and dance the lost meteor
invented a wing for your anguish

the two lines of beginning and end
singing drew closer in space—

Your century
a weeping willow
overhung incomprehensible things

Stones you carried
you paved
and broke up again
the font of wounds
and again you carried
that was the way
the death-commanded
martyr's way—

You lifted on to your shoulders
a point in the universe
in which human speech
sleeps the day through
and delicate as a soul
the sun loses its gold
in your hand you took the stone
which lives the interior dance
and makes night crumble to dust
where the nameless journey begins—

. . . .

Every pace closer to you
but morning a blossoming sojourn—
Night anointed regally deathly
Hurrying over sleeping sand
black meridian of trickling distance
wound about truth—

Hell is naked with pain—
Seeking
speechless
seeking
Crossing into the raven night
girt with all the Floods
and Ice Ages
to paint air
with that which grows behind the skin
Pilot beheaded with the knife of departure
Hum of sea shell drowns
Su Su Su

But between earth and sky
unchanged as ever the psalms pray
turn in their quivers of radiant dust—
And the divers with divine salutations
find no orphaned realm
in the rose-red woods of the deep—

When at last
behind the ear
in the death-vein
will my sightless universe
lie down to rest—

The blood's circulation
weeps toward
its spiritual sea
there
where the blue flame
of agony
bursts through night—

Lilies on the equator of anguish
When with your hands
you pronounced the blessing
distances contracted
those akin to the sea
drifted toward the beyond
and dust without memory began to flow—

When your jaw dropped
with the weight of earth—

III

In my room
where my bed stands
a table a chair
the kitchen stove
the universe kneels as everywhere
to be redeemed
from invisibility—
I draw a line
write down the alphabet
paint on the wall the suicidal words
that make the newborn burgeon at once
I have just fastened the planets to truth
when the earth begins to hammer
night works loose
drops out
dead tooth from the gum—

This is an excursion to a place
where the shadows sign other contracts—
you sit turned away from me
your back moves through night
your talk with the other side is mute
prophecies—pale lightning
on the wall of ashes

There's much dying out there in the greenness
You are sandy nearness out there in your graves—

And you walked over death
like a bird in snow
always blackly sealing the end—
Time gulped down
whatever you gave it of parting
right to the utmost forsaking
along the fingertips
night of eyes
To grow bodiless
The air was washed all round by—
an ellipse—the street of pains—

Then alone
with the shivering wing
like men in polar ice
where always there is a supernumerary One—
the mourning-cloak night
has a wound
won't cover me—

Am in strange parts
protected by the 8
the holy looped angel
He is always on his way
through our flesh
creating unrest
and making dust ripe for flying—

And I think of her
in the delirium of falling
whose child re-created her out of air
"your right leg bird-light—
your left leg bird-light—
tooee tooee—
Call in the south wind
Hearts like water can tremble in one's hand
like water tremble
Eyelid held open by depth—"

I saw him step from the house
the fire had singed
but not burned him
He carried a briefcase of sleep
under one arm
heavy inside with letters and figures
a whole arithmetic—
Into his arm was branded:
7337 the ruling number
These numbers had conspired among themselves
The man was a surveyor
Already his feet were rising from the earth
One was waiting for him above
to build a new paradise
"Only wait—you too will soon be at rest—"

Captive everywhere
the street that I walk
the vehicles I avoid
Put away the things I have bought
all visionary excursions into your realms—
My foot trips—hurts
a detour into your dwellings—
Deborah was stabbed by stars
and yet sang triumphant hymns
when the mountains dissolved
and on white-gleaming donkeys like prophets
the troop of horsemen moved on

But silence is where the victims dwell—

A game like blindman's bluff
on the green meadow
when the virgins pursued
hunted by deadly panic
climbed on to trees
that grew into the sky
and they plunged into the void
the sevenfold constellation
lost the tear
in the orphans' colony—

Who can hide
like a river in the sea
or bend night
brazenly sleeping
into the white fire
that writes "Open"
when earth is five inches of misery
beneath her creator—

Not HERE nor THERE
but double-tongued in sleep
Nature stammers out her decline
the shadow goes home
The planet rambles along the lines of life
sucking in regal messages
grows richer—

They collided in the street
Two destinies on this earth
Two circulations of blood in their arteries
Two that breathed on their way
in this solar system
Over their faces a cloud passed
time had cracked
Remembrance peered in
The far and the near had fused
From past and future
two destinies glittered
and fell apart—

Leave without looking back—
tear the last quaking-grass from your eyes
When Tsong-kha-pa left his master
he did not turn to look
Departure dwelt in his stride
Time flared up from his shoulders—

The man left behind cried out:
"Throw his hovel into the chasm—"
And the hovel floated above the chasm
shot through with five-hued light—
And he of no parting strode
into the cropped place that is pure spirit
And his house was no longer a house
Only light—

Faster time faster
when the second second forces the first to its knees
the golden army all day long on the march
in haste
till at evening all have been beaten
a rosemary bush the sky
night washes death down to its primal color
the elements sick with nostalgia break loose
run to the sea
grow breathless
refuse to blossom
for another has died
who took time's measure—

I write you—
You have come into the world again
with the haunting strength of letters
that groped for your essence
Light shines
and your fingertips glow in the night
Constellation at the birth
of darkness like these verses—

Pull over oneself
sleep the blanket of seven sleepers
Hide with seals
that in the wound which was exiled
and ram-lightning of the Last Judgment—
But only the word lashed bloody
breaks into resurrection
the soul on its wing—

Dark hissing of the wind
in the corn
The victim ready to suffer
The roots are still
but the ears of corn
know many native languages—

And the salt in the sea
weeps afar
The stone is a fiery being
and the elements tug on their chains
to be united
when the ghostly script of the clouds
fetches home primal images

Mystery on the border of death
"Lay a finger upon your lips:
Silence Silence Silence"—

. . . .

Four days four nights
a coffin was your hiding place
Survival breathed in—breathed out—
to delay death—
Between four boards
lay the world's anguish—

Outside grew the minute full of flowers
over the sky clouds played—

Thrown the seed grain's mystery
already strikes root in the future
begins:
A dance in the Ardennes
subterranean seeking
for the face in the rock crystal
Dawn in the Nothingness above
the South Sea
Lovers
hold to their ears the conch
with the deep-sea concert
A star opens to an entrance
The moon has had visitors
The old man does not return
A birth sucks at life—

IV

Despair
your letters like matchsticks
spewing fire
No one reaches his end
but through your branched antler words

Disconsolate site
place of lucid madness
before darkness falls
Straggler of life
and pioneer of dying
with no haven
Sweeping need
Grazing the mystery of
the invisible Messiah
with a wild craving for home—

We rushed
into the dungeon of parting
backwards
shadow-black already
given over
to the extinguished—

....

The sea
gathers moments
knows nothing of eternity
knots
the Cloth of Four Winds
in ecstasy
Tiger and cricket
sleep in the lullaby
of wet time—

The music
that you heard
was an alien music
Your ear was turned outward—
A sign claimed your attention
devoured your range of vision
cooled your blood
made you feel hidden
averted the lightning flash from your shoulder blade
You heard
something new

How many blinkings of eyelashes
when horror came
no eyelid to be lowered
and a heap of time put together
painted over the air's humility

This can be put on paper only
with one eye ripped out—

You painted the signal
red with your blood
warning of destruction
moist on the borders
but still without birth

When suffering settles homeless
it expels superfluity
Tears are orphans—expelled
in one bound we follow
that is flight into the Beyond
of the rootless palm tree of time—

Once
when in the redness evening forgot the day
I founded
the future upon the stone of sadness

Prenatal reunion—
a time made of ocean
ran its course—

Perhaps near the equator a fish
on the line paid off a human debt
and then my Thou
who was kept a prisoner
and whom to release I was chosen
and whom in enigmas I lost once more
until hard silence descended on silence
and a love was granted its coffin—

So briefly delivered up is humankind
who then can speak of love
the ocean has longer words
and so has the crystal-fanned Earth
with prophetic growth
This suffering paper
sick already with the Song of Dust to Dust
carrying off the blessed word
perhaps back to its magnetic point
which is permeable by God—

One must not permit oneself
to suffer *so*
said the seer of Lublin
and every word
crisscrossed with midnight
sleeplessly turned over
you heard elsewhere
perhaps
where a measure was found for immoderation
Love freed from earthly matter
the language of meteors
forbidden to a star
and you yourself were beside yourself
you seer of Lublin—

These millennia
blown by the breath
always in orbit around an angry noun
out of the sun's beehive
stinging seconds
warlike aggressors
secret torturers

Never a breathing space as in Ur
when a people of children tugged at the white ribbons
to play sleep-ball with the moon—

In the street with wind's haste
the woman runs
to fetch medicine for the sick child

Vowels and consonants
cry out in every language:
H e l p !

I'm on the track of my rights of domicile
this geography of nocturnal countries
where the arms opened for love
hang crucified on the degrees of latitude
groundless in expectation—

It is a black like
chaos before the word
Leonardo looked for that black
behind black
Job was swaddled
in the life-bearing body of the stars
Someone shakes the blackness
till the apple Earth drops
ripened to its end
A sigh
is that the soul—?

Always on the tilted plane
where everything falls away—rolls
into the abyss
the moving-standing word
mortally struck by silence
and the seed grain of night
bursts open again
amid the new language's tremor
whispered into
the root leaves of the planet
before sunrise—

The outrushing
torchlight procession of ancestors
in the hyssop gardens their heads glittered
in the blood's hiding places fleeing the country the God
On the shores of midnight
on the banished islands
baptized with the weather vanes of lightning
Agony in burning temples
Your home removed into my arteries—

Rich I am as the ocean
of past and future
and wholly of mortal stuff
I sing your song—

EDITORS' NOTE

Nelly Sachs' "Glowing Enigmas" first appeared in Michael Hamburger's English translation in the United States in two separate volumes, *O the Chimneys* (Farrar, Straus, and Giroux, 1967) and *The Seeker* (Farrar, Straus, and Giroux, 1970), both of which are now out of print. Parts I, II, and III of "Glowing Enigmas" appeared in *O the Chimneys*; part IV appeared in *The Seeker*. Never before has this poem appeared in its entirety in English as a single volume. All line, stanza, and section breaks used in this edition of *Glowing Enigmas* are based on the Swedish Academy and Nobel Foundation's German-language presentation copy of Nelly Sachs' collected works (printed under the title *Nobelpris für Literatur*) published in 1966 by Coron-Verlag (Zurich) in association with Suhrkamp Verlag (Frankfurt) and les Édtions Rombaldi (Paris).

Tavern Books offers its sincerest thanks to Richard Hamburger and The Michael Hamburger Trust. Without the help of Richard Hamburger, this publication would not have been possible.

ABOUT THE AUTHOR

Nelly Sachs was born in Berlin on December 10, 1891. At the age of forty-eight, in 1940, she fled Nazi Germany as a passenger on one of the last planes allowed to carry Jewish civilians out of the country. As an exile in Sweden, Nelly Sachs began to write because, as she attested, language was all she had left. Her first volume of poetry, *In den Wohnungen des Todes* (*In the Houses of Death*), 1947, confronted the suffering and persecution she witnessed. Other books followed: *Sternverdunkelung* (*Eclipse of Stars*), 1949, *Und niemand weiss weiter* (*And No One Knows Where to Go*), 1957, and *Flucht und Verwandlung* (*Flight and Metamorphosis*), 1959. Sachs' work became increasingly mystic and internal as she struggled with giving voice to the lost. Of her own poetry, she said, "My metaphors are my wounds." Sachs lived alone in Stockholm in a four-square-meter apartment, where she wrote *Glowing Enigmas* during the 1960s. Sachs was awarded the 1966 Nobel Prize for Literature. Her seventy-fifth birthday was the day of the ceremony. Nelly Sachs died May 12, 1970.

ABOUT THE TRANSLATOR

Michael Hamburger was born in Berlin in 1924 to a German-Jewish family that emigrated to England in 1933. He served as an infantryman from 1943 to 1947, and read Modern Languages at Oxford. After an academic career in England and America, he settled in Suffolk. In addition to his international renown as a poet and scholar, Hamburger is regarded as one of the great literary translators of his generation. Among the numerous authors he translated into English are Charles Baudelaire, Gottfried Benn, Bertolt Brecht, Paul Celan, Hans Magnus Enzensberger, Johann Wolfgang von Goethe, Friedrich Hölderlin, Rainer Maria Rilke, W. G. Sebald, and Georg Trakl. His acclaimed critical study *The Truth of Poetry* was published in 1968. His *Collected Poems* (Anvil, 1995), drawing on some twenty earlier books, has been followed by five more. His final book of poems, *Circling the Square*, was published by Anvil in 2007, the year of his death.

ABOUT THE ARTIST

Sarah Horowitz lives in Portland, Oregon, and is currently a member of Atelier Mars printmaking workshop. Her ink drawing, *Chrysalis* (2011), which appears on the cover, was commissioned by Tavern Books. Along with prints and drawings, she produces limited-edition artist books under her imprint Wiesedruck. Her books combine her own prints and the text, poetry, or other writings by select artists including Paul Celan, Kadya Molodowsky, Sarah Lantz, and Paul Auster. She was recently a resident at Frans Masreel Centrum for printmaking in Kasterlee, Belgium, and has received two project grants from the Regional Arts and Culture Council, Oregon. Her prints and drawings are represented by Froelick Gallery in Portland, Oregon, and Armstrong Fine Art in Chicago, Illinois. Horowitz's work can be found in collections internationally, including those in Frans Masereel Centrum (Belgium), Harvard University Houghton Library, Jewish Theological Seminary Library, Library of Congress, New York Public Library, Princeton University Firestone Library, Smith College, University of Alberta, and Yale University, among numerous others.

TAVERN BOOKS

Tavern Books is a 501(c)(3) not-for-profit charitable organization that exists to print, promote, and preserve works of literary vision, to foster a climate of cultural preservation, and to disseminate books in a way that benefits the reading public. In addition to reviving out-of-print books, we publish works in translation from the world's finest poets. We keep our titles in print, honoring the cultural contract between publisher and author, as well as between publisher and public. Our catalog, known as The Living Library, sustains the visions of our authors, ensuring their voices are alive in the social and artistic discourse of our modern era.

THE LIVING LIBRARY

Arthur's Talk with the Eagle by Anonymous,
translated from the Welsh by Gwyneth Lewis

Ashulia by Zubair Ahmed

Buson: Haiku by Yosa Buson,
translated from the Japanese by Franz Wright

*Poems 1904 by C. P. Cavafy,
translated from the Greek by Paul Merchant

**Evidence of What is Said: The Correspondence between
Charles Olson and Ann Charters*
with photographs by Ann Charters

*Who Whispered Near Me by Killarney Clary

The End of Space by Albert Goldbarth

Six-Minute Poems: The Last Poems
by George Hitchcock

*The Wounded Alphabet: Collected Poems Vol. 1
by George Hitchcock

*The Wounded Alphabet: Collected Poems Vol. 2
by George Hitchcock

*The Boy Changed into a Stag Clamors
at the Gate of Secrets* by Ferenc Juhász,
translated from the Hungarian by David Wevill

*My Blue Piano by Else Lasker-Schüler,
translated from the German by Eavan Boland

Archeology by Adrian C. Louis

*Fire Water World and *Among the Dog Eaters*
by Adrian C. Louis

Ocean by Joseph Millar

(continued)

Winterward by William Stafford

Baltics by Tomas Tranströmer
with photographs by Ann Charters,
translated from the Swedish by Samuel Charters

For the Living and the Dead by Tomas Tranströmer,
translated from the Swedish by John F. Deane

Prison by Tomas Tranströmer
with a postscript by Jonas Ellerström,
translated from the Swedish by Malena Mörling

Tomas Tranströmer's First Poems and
Notes From the Land of Lap Fever
by Tomas Tranströmer and with a commentary by Jonas Ellerström,
translated from the Swedish by Malena Mörling

Casual Ties by David Wevill

Collected Poems: Volume 1 by David Wevill

Collected Poems: Volume 2 by David Wevill

Collected Translations by David Wevill

Notes on Sea & Shore by Greta Wrolstad

The Countries We Live In by Natan Zach,
translated from the Hebrew by Peter Everwine

forthcoming

Tavern Books is funded, in part, by the generosity of philanthropic organizations, public and private institutions, and individual donors.

By supporting Tavern Books and its mission, you enable us to publish the most exciting poets from around the world and revive out-of-print works. Your contribution is essential in our effort to print, promote, and preserve the finest poetry books of our modern era.

MAJOR FUNDING HAS BEEN PROVIDED BY

Lannan Foundation

Lannan

THE PUBLICATION OF THIS BOOK WAS MADE POSSIBLE, IN PART, BY THE FOLLOWING INDIVIDUALS

Dean & Karen Garyet
Dorianne Laux and Joseph Millar
Marjorie Simon
Ron & Kathy Wrolstad

To learn more about underwriting Tavern Books titles, please contact us by e-mail: tavernbooks@gmail.com

COLOPHON

This book was designed and typeset by Michael McGriff. The text is set in Garamond, an old-style serif typeface named for the punch-cutter Claude Garamond (c. 1480-1561). Myriad, a humanist sans-serif typeface designed by Robert Slimbach and Carol Twombly, is used for the cover and displays. Printed on archival-quality paper at McNaughton & Gunn, Inc.

In addition to the paperback, an edition of 250 hardcovers has been printed. Twenty-six hardcovers have been signed and lettered A-Z by Sarah Horowitz.